C0-FYM-427

Robinson Crusoe

A Guide for
Teachers and Students

Classics for Young Readers

Sir Gibbie by George Macdonald
Sir Gibbie: A Guide for Teachers and Students
Hans Brinker by Mary Mapes Dodge
Hans Brinker: A Guide for Teachers and Students
A Little Princess by Frances Hodgson Burnett
A Little Princess: A Guide for Teachers and Students
Black Beauty by Anna Sewell
Black Beauty: A Guide for Teachers and Students
Robinson Crusoe by Daniel Defoe
Robinson Crusoe: A Guide for Teachers and Students

Robinson Crusoe

A Guide for
Teachers and Students

Ranelda Mack Hunsicker

P&R
PUBLISHING
P.O. BOX 817 • PHILLIPSBURG • NEW JERSEY 08865-0817

©2002 by Ranelda Mack Hunsicker

All rights reserved. Except for brief quotations for the purpose of review or comment and except for educational use (see below), no part of this book may be reproduced, stored in a retrieval system, or transmitted in any form or by any means—without the prior permission of the publisher, P&R Publishing Company, P.O. Box 817, Phillipsburg, New Jersey 08865-0817

A teacher who purchases one copy of this book may photocopy the entire book up to five times for use in her own classroom without requesting permission. Charging for copies or otherwise using them for commercial use is strictly prohibited.

Design by Tobias Design
Typesetting by Michelle Feaster

Printed in the United States of America

ISBN 0-87552-736-1

Contents

To Parents and Teachers . . .

Mark Twain once said, "A classic is something that everybody wants to have read and nobody wants to read." All too frequently this is true because the enduring power of the classics is lost in tedious classroom assignments. Books that could be savored become drudgery. To help you and your young reader avoid this pitfall, we encourage you to use this study guide wisely and creatively. Here are some issues to keep in mind:

- **Vocabulary Building.** Reluctant readers may benefit by studying the vocabulary words in advance of each reading assignment. This provides them with greater reading confidence and less distraction from the story. More gifted readers will know many of the vocabulary words or will deduce their meaning from the text itself. For definitions of vocabulary words, consult *Webster's New Collegiate Dictionary.*
- **Comprehension Questions.** Alternate between having students respond to questions orally and in writing. If a student can't answer a particular question, don't belabor it. Keep a list of the more challenging questions for further reflection and return to them later to see if understanding has blossomed. Don't expect a pat answer to every question. Many of the questions are intended to draw out personal opinions and theories, important skills for a maturing mind.
- **Story Continuity.** Do not interrupt an especially satisfying reading session by stopping at the end of each chapter to do the study guide exercises. Sometimes it is best to read several chapters at a time, saving the exercises for a natural pause in the flow of the plot.

- **Group Interaction.** The whole family or class can enjoy this classic story together. Whenever possible, adults and young readers should take turns reading pages or chapters aloud. Then spend a few minutes responding to the story and to one another's thoughts and feelings. Looking back on years of teaching, author and educator Aidan Chambers observes, "It was booktalk that pumped blood into our literary veins and gave us the energy, the impetus, for exploration beyond our familiar boundaries." Be sure to make time in your home and classroom for plenty of stimulating booktalk.
- **Creative Activities.** Intersperse vocabulary and comprehension building with the more expressive activities at the end of the study guide. These activities help students move from understanding the story to responding at a more personal level, a key element in internalizing and applying truth.
- **Assignments.** This guide is designed to encourage discussion between teachers and students. Students should have a notebook in which to keep completed vocabulary exercises and answers to study questions. This will maintain a permanent record of what they have learned from *Robinson Crusoe*.
- **Knowledge Tests and Answer Key.** In addition to questions for reflection and discussion, this guide supplies tests with short answers ideal for pop quizzes. The answer key in the back of the guide makes it easy for parents and teachers to check student work.

As you begin this reading adventure, keep in mind these words of award-winning children's author Katherine Paterson: "The gift of creative reading, like all natural gifts, must be nourished or it will atrophy. And you nourish it [as] you read, think, talk, look, listen, hate, fear, love, weep—and bring all of your life like a sieve to what you read."

Meet the Author: Daniel Defoe (1660–1731)

What would you do if you were born into a prosperous but persecuted family? Daniel Defoe faced this challenge from birth. His parents were Puritans at a time when these devout Protestants had lost their control of England's government. His father was a successful London merchant, but the family's religious beliefs made them social outsiders. Young Daniel could have rejected his parents' faith. He could have felt sorry for himself and become lazy, wild, or self-indulgent. Instead, he chose a life of discipline and quiet courage, and he had amazing adventures.

At the age of five young Daniel lived through England's Plague Year. When he was six, most of the great city of London burned to the ground, including all but three houses in the Defoes' neighborhood. It was a rough beginning for a boy, but then he was blessed with a wonderful minister-teacher. This godly man taught him how to think and write clearly and how to use stories to help people understand the truth.

After getting his education, Daniel followed in his father's footstep as a merchant. He wasn't much good at it because he was far more interested in politics than business. As a young man, he fought in a rebellion against King James II. He wanted to help William of Orange, a Dutch Protestant, become king of England. Defoe found he had more talent as a spy and political writer than as a soldier. Unfortunately, his writings and his business debts sent him to prison twice before he was forty.

Defoe was especially sad and ashamed that he had lost all of his wife's money. He loved her deeply and they had seven children who must have suffered from their father's problems. But Defoe didn't give up on life. He found comfort in his strong Christian faith, prayer, his family, and writing. In the early 1700s he became Britain's leading journalist, writing and publishing several successful newspapers. At the same time, he served his country for more than ten years as a spy. He was known as "an utterly independent man who could not be bullied or bought."

Defoe had always loved adventure stories set in faraway places, especially stories about shipwrecks and marooned sailors. When he was almost sixty, he decided to try writing a sea adventure and the result was *Robinson Crusoe*. It was his first novel and a huge success. By the end of the year it was published—1719—it had been translated into French, German, and Dutch. It is estimated that Defoe made about £325 for *Robinson Crusoe* and its sequels (about $33,300 today).

In his final years, Daniel Defoe compared his life to an ocean voyage. He wrote, "I am so near my journey's end, and am hastening to the place where the weary are at rest, and where the wicked cease to trouble; be it that the passage is rough, and the day stormy, by what way soever He pleases to bring me to the end of it, I desire to finish life with this temper [attitude] of soul in all cases: Te Deum Laudamus [We praise You, God]."

Chapter 1

THE FAMILY LEFT BEHIND

Part 1: What's in a Word?

Here are some words that may be new to you. You may be able to guess their meanings by looking at the way they are used in the story. Check in a dictionary to see if your guess is correct.

1. merchant
2. lieutenant
3. regiment
4. gout
5. calamity
6. insufficient
7. prophetic
8. repent
9. proposal
10. allurement

Part 2: Think about It . . .

1. Sometimes writers tell their stories from one person's viewpoint. Sometimes they switch from one person's viewpoint to that of another person. Sometimes they allow readers to see things from outside the characters, looking on as God does. What viewpoint did Defoe choose to tell the story of Robinson Crusoe?

2. What might have caused Robinson's family to change their name from Kreutznaer to Crusoe? What do you think is the most likely reason for the change?
3. Robinson's father believed that being poor or being rich usually led to unhappiness. Does the Bible teach this? (Hint: Proverbs 30:8–9.) Can you think of some examples to support Mr. Crusoe's opinion?
4. What struggle went on inside Robinson's mind and heart?
5. Why was it easy for Robinson to sail away with his friend without telling his family?

Chapter 2

FIRST ADVENTURES AT SEA

Part 1: What's in a Word?

Match the following words with their definitions.

1. ___ trough	a. God's direction and protection
2. ___ vow	b. upright pole on a ship
3. ___ prodigal	c. wasteful; wanderer; wicked
4. ___ conscience	d. ship
5. ___ mast	e. dip; channel
6. ___ boatswain	f. sailing; steering
7. ___ hazard	g. promise; pledge
8. ___ token	h. sign; warning
9. ___ Providence	i. honesty; goodness
10. ___ vessel	j. sense of right and wrong

11. ___ integrity — k. officer in charge of a ship's hull and equipment

12. ___ navigation — l. danger

Part 2: Think about It . . .

1. In what way was Robinson Crusoe like a wave of the sea?
2. Did the storm cause Crusoe to have a true change of heart? How can you tell?
3. What kind of person was Crusoe's friend?
4. Crusoe's experience is compared to two Bible stories, one in the Old Testament and one in the New Testament. What are the two stories?
5. What was the difference between Crusoe's desire to go to sea and the seafaring life of the ship's owner?
6. Was Crusoe ashamed for the right or wrong reason? Explain.

Chapter 3

IN AND OUT OF SLAVERY

Part 1: What's in a Word?

Use each of the following words in a sentence of your own.

1. rigging
2. stark
3. headway
4. perish
5. deliverance

Part 2: Think about It . . .

1. Calculate in United States currency how much money Crusoe had as he set sail with the new captain. (For online help, go to http://www.x-rates.com/calculator.html.)
2. Using a map of Africa and its coasts, locate the Canary Islands and Sallee (now called Salé), home of the Turkish pirates who captured Crusoe. What ocean was Crusoe in?
3. Crusoe mentions the Moors. Who were they? (Hint: You can learn about them in any encyclopedia.)
4. What did you learn in this chapter about Crusoe? List at least three qualities he showed.
5. Did Crusoe treat Xury as his equal? Describe their relationship.

Chapter 4

FROM BRAZIL TO A SHIPWRECK

Part 1: What's in a Word?

Circle the **wrong** *definition from the choices given:*

1. inventory

   a. list b. record c. sketch

2. ducat

   a. coin b. gem c. gold piece

3. passage

   a. ship b. transportation c. labor

4. liken

   a. compare b. adjust c. make equal

5. preposterous

   a. fortunate   b. ridiculous   c. foolish

6. ravenous

   a. birdlike   b. wild   c. starved

Part 2: Think about It . . .

1. Why did Crusoe sell Xury, in spite of the kindness the boy had shown?
2. What made Crusoe decide to become a planter in Brazil?
3. Why did Crusoe attempt another voyage to Africa? (Hint: The answer to these first three questions is basically the same.)
4. How do Robinson Crusoe's choices and experiences illustrate what the Bible tells us in 1 Timothy 6:9–10?

Chapter 5

LOOTING THE WRECKED SHIP

Part 1: What's in a Word?

Use the following words to fill in the blanks in the sentences below them.

abate	rummaging	gale
resolved	leagues	drainage
inlet	barricade	plain
forecastle	hogshead	fortifies

1. Between the two mountain ranges we saw a ________________, as smooth and flat as an enormous table.

2. I hope the storm will _______________ so our soccer game won't be canceled.
3. Tom steered his rowboat into the narrow _______________ and sailed safely to his uncle's dock.
4. "I've never seen such a huge _______________!" the sailor exclaimed as he struggled to load the barrel on board.
5. The marshy land was considered worthless until farmers built canals that provided proper _______________.
6. "Stand guard in the _______________," the captain told his first mate. He immediately hurried to the front of the first deck.
7. We _______________ to ride out the storm, letting the _______________ wind push us where it would.
8. We put a _______________ around our tent, but it didn't keep animals from _______________ through our supplies and stealing our food.
9. A healthy person should be able to walk two or three _______________ in a day.
10. Eating several servings of fruits and vegetables each day _______________ us against many illnesses.

Part 2: Think about It . . .

1. Did Robinson Crusoe have a right to loot the ship? Why or why not?
2. What made the chest of carpenter's tools more valuable than a shipload of gold?
3. How can you tell that Crusoe was not hopeless about his situation?
4. What did Crusoe mean when he said, "O drug! what are you good for?"

Test your knowledge of Chapters 1–5 by answering these questions. (See back of guide for answers.)

1. What did Robinson Crusoe's father want him to do for a living?
2. What did Crusoe want to do instead?
3. What happened to the first ship on which Crusoe sailed?
4. Where did Crusoe go on his next voyage?
5. Who made Crusoe a slave?
6. Who was Xury?
7. Where did Crusoe go to live after he escaped?
8. What caused Crusoe to return to sea?
9. What happened to Crusoe's shipmates?
10. What did Crusoe find onboard the wrecked ship that he could not use at all?

Chapter 6

MAKING A HOME

Part 1: What's in a Word?

Mark each sentence below with a ★ [star] if the vocabulary word is used correctly and the sentence makes sense. Mark the sentence with an X if the word is used incorrectly.

___ 1. Our teacher used several facts to **fortress** his belief that God created the universe.

___ 2. If you are worried about a problem you can't solve, it helps to **divert** your thoughts with work or play.

___ 3. We surprised Dad with a backyard **hammock** where he can rest after mowing the grass.

___ 4. **Latitude** is measured by parallel lines running top to bottom on a map.

___ 5. Ben felt **desolate** when his best friend moved to another state.

___ 6. I must go shopping for groceries because we have a **sufficient** supply.

___ 7. Mom provides **alternatives** to junk food so that we can make healthy choices.

___ 8. A **terrace** is designed to provide safety and defense.

___ 9. "You'll find your new baseball glove in that **parcel** on the right," my grandmother said and pointed to a brightly wrapped package.

___10. Our new classmate is Swedish and has **acquaint** accent.

Part 2: Think about It . . .

How did Crusoe shake off despair? What attitude did he have about his situation?

Chapter 7

GETTING ORGANIZED

Part 1: What's in a Word?

Write down one word that means about the same thing as:

1. navigation
2. devise
3. banish

4. miraculous
5. barren
6. enable
7. application (as used in this chapter)
8. folly

Part 2: Think about It . . .

1. What difference did it make whether Robinson Crusoe forgot which day was the Sabbath?
2. What advantage was it for Crusoe to organize his things so carefully?
3. How does Crusoe's story show that determination is more important than knowledge or skill?
4. Use Crusoe's example to make a list of your miseries and comforts. (Note to teacher: Allow student to keep this list confidential if he or she chooses.)

Chapter 8

DIARY OF A CASTAWAY

Part 1: What's in a Word?

Match the following words with their definitions.

1. ___ necessities	a. lever
2. ___ comrades	b. excite; awaken
3. ___ shoal	c. hole into which something fits
4. ___ habitation	d. rushes; reeds with large leaves
5. ___ tolerable	e. sign

6.	___ crowbar	f.	give
7.	___ socket	g.	cement
8.	___ mortar	h.	needs; essential things
9.	___ flags	i.	numb; in shock
10.	___ hinder	j.	nourishment; food
11.	___ endeavor	k.	shallow water; sandbar
12.	___ sustenance	l.	friends; coworkers
13.	___ evidence	m.	fair; acceptable
14.	___ stupefied	n.	delay; prevent
15.	___ rouse	o.	dwelling place; home
16.	___ bestow	p.	try; attempt

Part 2: Think about It . . .

1. In this chapter, Crusoe repeats many things he has told about in the previous chapters. Which is more enjoyable to read, his narrative (story) or his journal entries? Why?
2. In chapter 7, Crusoe showed a positive attitude. Chapter 8 tells us more about his attitude. Was it one of genuine gratitude to God? Did he believe God cared about him in a personal way and was involved in his life? How can you tell?

Chapter 9

A TURNING POINT

Part 1: What's in a Word?

Circle the best answer from the choices given.

1. Repentance is:

   a. feeling ashamed   b. sorrow over one's sin

2. If you look **seaward**, you turn your eyes:

   a. toward the water b. away from the water

3. When an animal acts on **instinct**, its behavior is:

   a. automatic b. carefully thought out

4. The **dictates** of common sense are:

   a. rules, laws, principles b. mistakes

5. **Ecstasy** is a feeling of:

   a. delight b. confusion

6. A person without a **conscience** does not have:

   a. friends b. a sense of right and wrong

Part 2: Think about It . . .

1. In what way did Crusoe's illness change his attitude?
2. Have you ever had a dream that helped you realize you needed to change something in your life?
3. What do you think Crusoe meant when he said he had been overwhelmed by "stupidity of soul"?
4. Read the story of Jonah in the Old Testament. What did Jonah and Robinson Crusoe have in common?

Chapter 10

FINDING COMFORT

Part 1: What's in a Word?

Use the following words to write a paragraph. Check the meaning of each word in a dictionary to make sure you have used it correctly.

1. govern
2. glorify
3. remission
4. humility
5. Savior

Part 2: Think about It . . .

1. How did God speak to Robinson Crusoe before he read the Bible?
2. In what ways is the Bible God's most trustworthy way of speaking to people?
3. Crusoe writes about two Bible verses in this chapter, Psalm 50:15 and Acts 5:31. Read these verses in two or three different Bible translations. Then write a sentence or two about what each verse means.
4. How did Crusoe's ideas about deliverance change?

Test your knowledge of Chapters 6-10 by answering these questions.

1. What animal on the island was Crusoe's main source of meat?
2. What kind of home did Crusoe first live in?
3. How did Crusoe keep a record of what happened on the island?
4. Had Crusoe ever used tools or built things before coming to the island?
5. What crops did Crusoe raise on the island?
6. Why couldn't Crusoe make broth?
7. What surprising source of eggs did Crusoe discover?
8. What encouraged Crusoe to repent of his sins?

9. What book did Crusoe read every day?
10. How many seasons did Crusoe's island have?
11. What was the best part of Crusoe's winter food?
12. How did Crusoe hide his first dwelling?

Chapter 11

EXPLORING THE ISLAND

Part 1: What's in a Word?

1. What is the difference between an **island** and a **continent**?
2. What is the difference between **broth** and **stew**?
3. What is the difference between **gunpowder** and **gunshot**?

Part 2: Think about It . . .

Why was it important for Robinson Crusoe to keep making new discoveries in spite of the danger involved in exploring his island?

Chapter 12

A NEW PET

Part 1: What's in a Word?

Circle the best definition for each word:

1. solitary

   a. alone   b. simple

2. civilization
   a. manners   b. community
3. isolation
   a. fear   b. loneliness
4. abominable
   a. hateful   b. conceited
5. anguish
   a. sorrow   b. hardness

Part 2: Think about It . . .

1. Crusoe said that, with God's help, he could be happier on the island than in civilization. Do you know anyone who spends most of his or her time alone but is still joyful? How is this possible?
2. What is the difference between Crusoe being thankful for being on the island and being thankful for what he learned on the island? Is there something in your life that you aren't thankful for but you still see God using for your good?

Chapter 13

BAKING BREAD

Part 1: What's in a Word?

1. Name two kinds of workers who might use a **mortar** and **pestle**.
2. Name three things that have **husk** and **bran**.
3. Name two places you would be apt to find **calico**, **linen**, and **muslin**.
4. Name four uses for **earthenware**.

Part 2: Think about It . . .

How did Crusoe decide the amount of crops he should plant each year? Do you think he planned correctly? What could have made his plan go wrong?

Chapter 14

GREAT IMPROVEMENTS

Part 1: What's in a Word?

Write a simple definition for the following words.

1. mainland
2. inhabited
3. undermine
4. mallet
5. chisel
6. discontent
7. flourish
8. resigned

Part 2: Think about It . . .

1. In this chapter Crusoe learned an important principle taught by Jesus. Read Luke 14:28-31. How do these words of Jesus relate to Crusoe's experience with the canoe?
2. Perhaps you've seen bumper stickers that say, "He who dies with the most toys wins," or "She who dies with the most clothes wins." Does this agree with what Crusoe learned on the island? What do you think his bumper sticker might say?

3. According to Robinson Crusoe, the secret of contentment is __________. See if you can find a Bible verse that tells us this is true.
4. Crusoe compared his experiences to the way ravens fed Elijah. Read this Old Testament story (1 Kings 17:1-6). Then make a list of ways God provided for Crusoe. Did the mercy he received outweigh his sorrow?

Chapter 15

OCEAN DANGER

Part 1: What's in a Word?

The same word can be used in very different ways. Use each of the following words in two sentences, showing two different meanings. (Hint: Capitalizing one of them will give you another way to use it.)

1. point
2. rash
3. current
4. eddy
5. grapple
6. kid

Part 2: Think about It . . .

1. Crusoe described his island experience as a reign and a captivity. How could it be both?
2. When Crusoe thought the current would take him away from his island forever, he said, "We never

know how to value what we enjoy until we lose it." Write two to three paragraphs describing an experience that taught you this.

Chapter 16

A DAIRY FARM

Think about It . . .

Visit the library and check out *The New Goat Handbook* by Ulrich Jaudas (Barrons, 1989) or a similar book about raising dairy goats. Is Robinson Crusoe's story about his dairy farm believable based on the information you find?

Test your knowledge of Chapters 11-16 by answering these questions.

1. What did Crusoe make to hold his grain?
2. How many times a day did Crusoe read the Bible?
3. What did Crusoe fear most as the years went by?
4. What mistake did Crusoe make in building his first canoe?
5. Why did Crusoe need clothes even though he was alone on the island?
6. Who called "Robin Crusoe" to the lonely sailor?
7. What happened to Crusoe when he first tried to sail around his island?
8. How did Crusoe get milk, butter, and cheese?
9. When Crusoe ate his meals, who sat with him?
10. Where was Crusoe's "country home"?

Chapter 17

THE FOOTPRINT

Part 1: What's in a Word?

Match the following words with their definitions.

1. ___ fancied	a. kind; class
2. ___ presently	b. right away
3. ___ racked	c. replace; drive away
4. ___ banish	d. imagined
5. ___ founded	e. distant
6. ___ shun	f. avoid; ignore
7. ___ species	g. built; established
8. ___ stirred	h. tortured; troubled
9. ___ remote	i. moved

Part 2: Think about It . . .

1. Since Crusoe hated being alone, why was he so terrified by the footprint on the beach?
2. What does the Bible tell us about fear? (Hint: Joshua 1:9; Proverbs 29:25; John 14:27; 1 John 4:18)
3. When is fear a good thing? (Hint: Proverbs 1:7, 9:10; Hebrews 11:7)
4. Robinson Crusoe was comforted by this verse from the Old Testament: "Wait on the Lord, and be of good cheer, and He shall strengthen thy heart; wait, I say, on the Lord." Where are these words found? (Hint: A Bible concordance will help you find them.)

Chapter 18

CANNIBALS

Think about It . . .

1. How did Crusoe's fears hurt his conversations with God?
2. Crusoe thanked God that he had not been born a cannibal. Jesus told a story about a man who thanked God that he was not an evil person. You'll find the story in the New Testament in Luke 18:9-14. In what way was Crusoe like the Pharisee? In what way was he different?
3. Crusoe decided that the cannibals were not guilty of murder as he would be if he killed someone. What made the difference? Does God judge different people by different standards? (To answer the last question, you and your class or family may want to spend time studying Romans 2:1-16.)
4. Crusoe mentioned evil done by Spaniards against the native people of America. What was he talking about? How do people's attitudes about certain behavior and actions change over time?
5. Write a good rule for yourself about judging other people based on what the Bible teaches and what you learned from Crusoe's example.

Chapter 19

A SECRET CAVE

Part 1: What's in a Word?

Find a synonym for each of the following words based on the way they are used in chapter 19.

1. impression
2. intuition
3. intolerable
4. venture (noun)
5. grotto

Part 2: Think about It . . .

1. Robinson Crusoe believed in following his intuition. What was probably the source of the impressions that guided him? Is it always safe to trust our intuition? Why or why not? (Read Proverbs 2:1-11.)
2. When Crusoe talked about the particular evil that was most dreadful to him, to what was he referring?

Chapter 20

ANOTHER SHIPWRECK

Part 1: What's in a Word?

1. When and why does **ebb tide** occur?
2. When and why does **flood tide** occur?

Part 2: Think about It . . .

1. How many weeks was Crusoe in "a mood for murder"? Why was this a poor way to use his time? What important truth had he forgotten? (Hint: This truth gave him courage in the cave described in the previous chapter.) See Psalm 46:1 and Hebrews 13:5–6.
2. What is a modern example of Crusoe's statement that "one man's safety is another man's destruction"?

Chapter 21

WONDERFUL DREAM

Part 1: What's in a Word?

Draw a ship like one Robinson Crusoe might have sailed aboard or the one that wrecked in this chapter. Label each of its main parts, including the forecastle, mainmast, bowsprit, stern, and quarter.

Part 2: Think about It . . .

1. After well over twenty years on the island, why would Crusoe still have a great deal of rum?
2. What did Crusoe believe was "the general plague of mankind"? In what way was he a *monument* (lasting evidence or reminder) to it?
3. Although Crusoe had learned much about God and His ways, he didn't see the wrong in slavery. How could this be?
4. How did the shipwreck near Crusoe's island change his attitude? Why?

Test your knowledge of Chapters 17-21 by answering these questions.

1. What did Crusoe see on the beach that terrified him?
2. What did Crusoe say was his only sorrow on the island?
3. What was Crusoe's greatest enemy?
4. Who were the first visitors to Crusoe's island?
5. What did Crusoe make with goat's tallow?

6. Where did Crusoe decide to store his weapons and ammunition?
7. What caused the second shipwreck near Crusoe's island?
8. Who did Crusoe rescue from the shipwreck?
9. How many chests did Crusoe take from the wrecked ship?
10. Why did Crusoe want a native prisoner?

Chapter 22

FINDING FRIDAY

Part 1: What's in a Word?

Match the following word with their definitions.

1. ___ clamber	a. totally
2. ___ kindle	b. climb
3. ___ inclined	c. without limits
4. ___ beckon	d. killer
5. ___ executioner	e. ruined; torn up
6. ___ disposition	f. hard working
7. ___ stark	g. ability
8. ___ mangled	h. hand motion
9. ___ tolerate	i. set fire to; light
10. ___ hankering	j. preparation
11. ___ precaution	k. character; attitude
12. ___ capacity	l. permit; allow
13. ___ infinite	m. likely
14. ___ diligent	n. desire

Part 2: Think about It . . .

1. By what standards did Crusoe judge Friday's appearance?
2. What was Crusoe's opinion of Friday's abilities?
3. How did Crusoe account for the difference in opportunities experienced by Europeans like himself and "savages" like Friday? Did he think God was unfair? Why or why not? What do you think? (Be sure to read Job 40:1–5 and Romans 9:14–24.)

Chapter 23

FRIENDSHIP

Part 1: What's in a Word?

Use the following words to fill in the blanks in the sentences below them.

redeemed	delude	motivated
fraud	quench	reform
enmity	pardon	wrangling

1. I wasn't ________________ to ________________ my behavior until I realized how much I was hurting others and grieving God.
2. Please stop ________________ about things that aren't important and only cause ________________ between people who could be friends.
3. The governor gave the prisoner a full ________________ releasing her and giving her a new chance at life.

4. You can ________________ many arguments by speaking quietly and politely.
5. My uncle ________________ his watch by paying what he owed at the shop where he pawned it.
6. A person who commits ________________ tries to ________________ others into believing something that isn't true.

Part 2: Think about It . . .

1. Using the information Friday provided, locate the approximate location of Crusoe's island on a map.
2. Make a chart showing the main differences between Friday's native religion and Crusoe's Christianity.
3. How did Friday help Crusoe become a better Christian?

Chapter 24

ARRIVAL OF SAVAGES

Part 1: What's in a Word?

Use the following words in sentences of your own after you are sure you understand each word's meaning.

1. fluently
2. musing
3. obligation
4. suspicion
5. venture
6. affection
7. bough

8. posture
9. barbarous
10. meddle

Part 2: Think about It . . .

1. Why did Robinson Crusoe feel confused about his friendship with Friday, traveling to the mainland, and what to do about the cannibals who came to his island?
2. How did Friday prove his loyalty to Crusoe?

Chapter 25

RESCUING CAPTIVES

Part 1: What's in a Word?

Circle the best definition for each word.

1. consternation

   a. alarm b. anger c. peace
2. barrow

   a. tunnel b. pushcart c. sled
3. yearling

   a. young animal b. male goat c. female goat
4. goods

   a. money b. slaves c. merchandise
5. inborn

   a. natural b. reformed c. intelligent
6. square dealer

   a. fat trader b. fair person c. blockhead

7. abhor

   a. desire b. enjoy c. hate

8. sacraments

   a. church ceremonies b. church teachings

9. plunder

   a. rob b. kidnap c. rescue

10. insolent

    a. shy b. bold c. foreign

Part 2: Think about It . . .

1. What is the difference between a fowling piece and a musket?
2. What is the difference between a longboat and a canoe?
3. The Spaniard rescued by Crusoe said his fellow sailors might become bitter if there weren't enough to eat. He compared how they might feel and act to an Old Testament story. Read this story in Exodus 16. When God provided plenty of food, did it take care of people's bad attitudes and misbehavior?

Chapter 26

THE MUTINEERS

Part 1: What's in a Word?

Write a short definition for the following words.

1. comply
2. volley
3. mutiny

4. vain
5. contrivance
6. fortification
7. gallows
8. hoist
9. avail
10. confound

Part 2: Think about It . . .

Crusoe said he thought of a trick "which fit my purpose to a T." What does this mean? What is the source of the expression "fit to a T"? How many idioms (expressions belonging to a particular area or group of people; common phrases) can you think of in three minutes? Some people think idioms are so entertaining that they collect them. Take a look at Marvin Terban's books *Mad as a Wet Hen, Punching the Clock,* and *In a Pickle* (Houghton Mifflin), collections of funny idioms.

Chapter 27

HEADING HOME

Part 1: What's in a Word?

1. If you make an **appeal**, are you demanding something or requesting something?
2. If you **seize** a boat, are you taking it by force or measuring it?
3. If you **expostulate** with someone, are you mocking or reasoning with him or her?

4. If you are **penitent**, do you apologize with sorrow or scheme to get your own way?
5. If you **recruit** someone, are you gaining his help or dismissing him?
6. If you are in a **garrison**, are you in a storage room or a military fort?
7. If someone sips a bit of **cordial**, is he taking medicine or drinking punch?
8. If a **rogue** wants you to do business with him, should you trust him or avoid him?

Part 2: Think about It . . .

1. How did Robinson Crusoe and the English captain follow Jesus' advice to be "shrewd as snakes and as innocent as doves"?
2. In what ways was Crusoe the same as when he came to the island? In what ways had he changed?

Test your knowledge of Chapters 22–27 by answering these questions.

1. How many years had Crusoe been on the island before he rescued Friday?
2. What three things did Crusoe teach Friday right away?
3. Who was Benamuckee?
4. On what condition did Friday want to return to the mainland?
5. What nationality was the first sailor that Crusoe and Friday rescued from the cannibals?
6. What relative of Friday's was brought to the island as a prisoner?

7. What brought an English ship to Crusoe's island?
8. What title did the English captain give Crusoe?
9. How many prisoners did Crusoe leave on the island when he sailed home? How many actually stayed there?
10. How many years had Crusoe been away from England when he returned?

"Get Creative!" Activities

Make a large map showing the areas where Robinson Crusoe traveled. Draw a different colored line for each of his journeys.

★ ★ ★

Imagine that Robinson Crusoe's father or mother sent a letter to him in London. When the kind Portuguese captain returned to get Crusoe's money, he also got the letter and delivered it to Crusoe in Brazil. Write the letter.

★ ★ ★

The Portuguese captain paid Crusoe with pieces of eight. These old coins were also called Spanish milled dollars. As a historical detective, your job is to find out: 1. Why the coins were called pieces of eight, and 2. How pieces of eight came to be a favorite kind of money in colonial America.

★ ★ ★

Plan a special Robinson Crusoe feast for your family, using mainly foods that were available on the island. Decorate the table with an island theme. During the meal, ask each person at the table what he or she would enjoy and hate about being a castaway. Read aloud your favorite part of *Robinson Crusoe*.

Here are a couple of recipe suggestions for your menu:

Mushroom & Barley Soup

1 medium onion, diced
1 tablespoon unsalted butter
1/2 pound fresh mushrooms, sliced
4 cups vegetable stock
1/2 cup pearled barley
1/4 cup plus 2 tablespoons milk
1 tablespoon all purpose flour

1. In a heavy saucepan, melt butter over medium high heat.
2. Cook onions and mushrooms in the melted butter for 3–4 minutes, or until softened.
3. Add stock, barley, salt, and pepper to taste. Bring to a boil. Reduce heat to low and simmer for 30 minutes.
4. Combine milk and flour in a jar with a tight fitting lid and shake until blended.
5. Stir milk and flour mixture into barley mixture and simmer 15 minutes until slightly thickened. Serves 4.

Rice Yogurt Supreme

1 1/2 cups cooked rice
8 oz. cartoon of pineapple yogurt
3/4 cup crushed pineapple, well drained
2 bananas, diced

Combine all ingredients, chill well before serving. Serves 5-6.

★ ★ ★

Try making candles with an adult's help. You will need:

Old candles or paraffin
A few pieces of crayons for color
1 small container, such as a baby food jar

String for a wick
1 long nail

Tie the string onto the nail, and lay the nail across the top of the small can or baby food jar, with the string hanging down inside the container. Put the old candles and the crayons in a coffee can, and put the coffee can in a pan of water. Do not put the wax directly into the pan. Set the pan on the stove, and melt the wax over low heat. Then pour the melted wax into your small container. Once the wax hardens, cut the string, leaving a short wick to light. The candle is now ready to use.

★ ★ ★

Reread the story of Crusoe's escape from slavery in chapter 3. Write about his escape from the viewpoint of Ismael or Xury. How would one of them describe what happened?

★ ★ ★

Read other books about what it's like to be stranded on an island:

- *Adrift* (Viking, 1992) by Allan Baillie
- *The Coral Island* (1857; Puffin, 1982) by R. M. Ballantyne
- *The Island of the Blue Dolphin* (1960; Scott Foresman, 1987) by Scott O'Dell
- *Call It Courage* (1940; Scott Foresman, 1990) by Armstrong Sperry
- *The Cay* (1969; Avon, 1995) by Theodore Taylor
- *Swiss Family Robinson* (1813; Dover, 2001) by Johann David Wyss

Write a one- or two-page essay comparing Robinson Crusoe to the main character in one of these books.

★ ★ ★

Bring some fun to Crusoe's island by playing Tom Swifties. Tom Swift was the hero of a series of old children's books. Almost every remark the characters made had an adverb attached. For example: " 'I may,' Tom promised, rather indefinitely," or " 'Why?' asked Tom, wonderingly." The *Random House Dictionary of the English Language* describes a Tom Swiftie as a play on words that involves a punning relationship between the way an adverb describes how a speaker says something and the speaker's statement, as in "I know who turned off the lights," Tom hinted darkly. Here's a deserted island Swiftie: "I need some bread," said Crusoe crustily. See how many Swifties you can create for Crusoe and his friend Friday.

★ ★ ★

Watch a film version of *Robinson Crusoe* and compare it to the book. Some possibilities are:

- *The Adventures of Robinson Crusoe* (1953), starring Dan O'Herlihy
- *Robinson Crusoe* (1972), animated
- *Robinson Crusoe* (1996), starring Pierce Brosnan

★ ★ ★

Make a poster illustrating one of the following:

- The kinds of money mentioned in the story and their value
- The plants and animals of Crusoe's island
- Crusoe's bread-making process

★ ★ ★

When people plan a vacation, they often use travel brochures to learn about the places they might want to visit on their trips. Collect several travel brochures (available from travel agents or in the lobby of hotels). After looking at them carefully, create a travel brochure for Crusoe's island.

★ ★ ★

Ask twenty or more people, "What three books besides the Bible would you want to have with you on a deserted island?" Write down their responses. Which books are mentioned most often? Make a recommended reading list for island castaways.

★ ★ ★

Defoe gives us many journal entries for Robinson Crusoe. Now it's your turn to write several journal entries for Friday.

★ ★ ★

Many experts believe that Daniel Defoe based *Robinson Crusoe* on the adventures of Alexander Selkirk, a sailor who was marooned on Juan Fernandez Island. See what you can learn about Selkirk and his island at the library and/or on the Internet. Make a chart with two columns: 1. Similarities in Selkirk's and Crusoe's experiences, 2. Differences in Selkirk's and Crusoe's experiences.

★ ★ ★

What messages might Crusoe have placed in bottles in hopes that someone would find and read them? Write several. Then see if you can find out where the tides might have carried the bottles. You'll find some clues at:

- http://www.the-sea.org/flow.htm
- http://www.mos.org/oceans/motion/currents.html
- http://www.acl.lanl.gov/GrandChal/GCM/currents.html

★ ★ ★

In *Robinson Crusoe* we read about a shipboard mutiny and how sternly the captain and Crusoe dealt with the mutineers. Read about mutinies in the encyclopedia. What were the most common causes of mutinies? What was the usual punishment for mutiny? Is mutiny ever justified? (Hint: Before you answer the last question, be sure to read about the Amistad mutiny, online at http://amistad.mysticseaport.org, in *Amistad* by Walter Dean Myers, or in *Freedom's Sons: The True Story of the Amistad Mutiny* by Suzanne Jurmain.)

Have a classroom or family debate about whether mutiny is always wrong. Be sure to support your argument with facts, examples, and principles from the Bible. Here are some Scripture passages to help you decide if and when mutiny is wrong: Romans 13:1–7; Titus 3:1–2; 1 Peter 2:13–17; Exodus 1:15–21; 1 Samuel 22:17; Acts 4:18–19.

★ ★ ★

Make a timeline of Robinson Crusoe's life. Be sure to show major historical events that took place while he was living as well as events that happened to him.

★ ★ ★

What would life have been like for Crusoe if he had washed up on:

- One of the Faeroe Islands
- Buru Island
- Easter Island (Rapa Nui)
- Heard Island

Write a one-paragraph description of what Crusoe might have experienced in each of these places.

★ ★ ★

Design a survivor T-shirt for Robinson Crusoe, Friday, and the sailors they rescued.

★ ★ ★

You are a CNN TV news reporter who has traveled back by time machine to June 11, 1687. You are standing at the dock when Robinson Crusoe and his companions arrive. What ten questions would you ask them?

★ ★ ★

Find out as much as you can about the life of Daniel Defoe. Make a list of the ways he used his own experiences and beliefs in writing *Robinson Crusoe*.

★ ★ ★

Robinson Crusoe always paid special attention to each anniversary of his arrival on the island. Do you remember the date of an important event in your life besides your birthday? Ask ten to twenty people this question. What kinds of events do they recall each year?

★ ★ ★

Would you like to step into Robinson Crusoe's adventure? Tivola Publishing makes it possible with its CD-ROM simulation game. There are nine sites on the island to explore close-up, as well as eleven 360-degree panoramic views of the scenery. By clicking on items in the illustrations, you can collect tools, build things, and make fascinating discoveries. This game includes an interactive, read-along version of Defoe's novel, optional narration of the text, musical background, and sound effects. Appropriate for ages eight and up, Tivola's *Robinson Crusoe* is available in Windows and Macintosh format. For more details, visit www.tivola.com or www.amazon.com.

Robinson Crusoe
Summary for Parents and Teachers

Robinson Crusoe is probably the world's favorite adventure story. For more than 270 years, readers of all ages everywhere have been fascinated by the young fool who ran away from wealth, security, and family love for a rough life at sea—and came to his senses too late, alone on a tropical island. Alone except for cannibals, that is, and God. The story is packed with suspense, surprises, and setbacks, as well as warmth, wisdom, and wonder. Life is never quite the same again for a person who has read *Robinson Crusoe*.

Defoe's story focuses on Robinson Crusoe's experiences on an island near the Orinoco River of Venezuela. Adjusting to the primitive conditions by practicing self-reliance and ingenuity, he learns to make tools, shelters, bread, clothes, baskets, pottery, candles, and canoes. More importantly, he becomes a Christian. After twenty-five years of solitude, one Friday he saves a black man from cannibals and thus acquires an excellent companion, whom he names Friday. Later on, other shipwreck survivors join him, he eventually returns to England, and he has more adventures.

Few people are aware that the book is extremely long—475 pages of fine print in the 1885 edition. In modern editions, the second half of the book is omitted and the first half tends to leave out Crusoe's long struggle with God and his slow transformation as he studies and applies God's Word. As part of P&R's Classics for Young Readers Series, Kathryn Lindskoog has edited *Robinson Crusoe* for today's reader, faithfully preserving every detail of the original story while featuring an accelerated pace, updated terminology, and full-page illustrations to add to your reading pleasure.

KNOWLEDGE TESTS ANSWER KEY

Most of the questions in this study guide are purposely designed to encourage reflection, discussion, and written response. For these kinds of questions, it is impossible (and counterproductive) to provide pat answers. However, to aid you in creating pop quizzes, here is a key to chapter summary items in the guide.

Test for Chapters 1–5

1. become a lawyer
2. go to sea
3. It sank.
4. Africa (Guinea)
5. Turkish pirates
6. a slave boy
7. Brazil
8. slave trading
9. They drowned.
10. money

Test for Chapters 6–10

1. goat
2. a tent
3. He wrote in journal or diary.
4. no
5. barley and rice
6. He had no cooking pot.
7. turtle
8. sickness
9. the Bible
10. two
11. raisins
12. He put a hedge around it.

Test for Chapters 11–16

1. baskets
2. three
3. cannibals
4. He built it too far from the water.
5. protection from heat and sun
6. his pet parrot
7. He was pulled to sea by a strong current.
8. by milking goats
9. his pets: a parrot, a dog, and two cats
10. in the interior of the island

Test for Chapters 17–21

1. a footprint
2. lack of human companionship
3. fear
4. cannibals
5. candles
6. in a cave
7. rocks and ocean current
8. a dog
9. two
10. to guide him to the mainland

Test for Chapters 22–27

1. twenty-five
2. not to eat humans, to wear clothes, to make bread
3. Friday's god
4. He wanted Crusoe to go with him.
5. Spanish
6. his father
7. a mutiny
8. governor
9. five; three
10. thirty-five

Also from

KATHRYN LINDSKOOG & RANELDA MACK HUNSICKER

— *How to Grow a Young Reader* —

In an age of interactive electronic games, TV, videos, and the Internet… you can raise a book lover.

Reading opens up a lifetime of learning and delight to children. This treasury offers insights into over 1,800 books for readers of all ages.

SHAW BOOKS | ISBN: 0-87788-408-0
www.waterbrookpress.com

"*How to Grow a Young Reader* is thorough, up-to-date, deeply thoughtful, and thought-generating."

—LLOYD ALEXANDER, Newbery award–winning author of numerous children's books, including *The High King*

"*How to Grow a Young Reader* is a superb guide through the world of children's literature."

—PAUL MCCUSKER, executive producer of the Adventures in Odyssey audio dramas

---

AVAILABLE THROUGH YOUR LOCAL BOOKSTORE